The Last Line

A collection of poems

Ahmed Morsi

@2024 ΛEEH PRESS INC

Middle East Manager and Editor: Ahmed M. Shalaby

Cover Design: Mahmoud Assad

Translation: Translation: Ashraf Abdel Hamid Al Genbihy

The romantic poetry collection characterizes poetic imagery's beauty and feelings' sincerity. The poems address the concepts of love, loyalty, and longing within a deep emotional framework, where the poet expresses his love as a constant pulse that never fades as if it were a perfume that remains despite the passage of time. The poems shed light on feelings of nostalgia and longing for the beloved, embodying the beloved as a mirror of beauty and charm.

They also evoke natural images, such as roses, planets, and the sea, to symbolize tenderness, beauty, and eternity. The poems highlight the emotional relationship as a life journey of hopeful and romantic situations. The poem "The Last Line" ends with the idea of separation as a painful truth narrated in an elegant style that mixes pain and regret.

AEEH PRESS INC

Dedication

To those who gave love a meaning beyond words,

To those whose hearts blossomed with the spring of union and withered with the autumn of separation,

To a love story whose lines were written with tears of joy and ended with a final line of longing,

To those who taught us that love has a beginning and an end, but it remains immortal in memory,

I dedicate this collection to you as a testimony to the brilliance of the moment and the pain of the end.

Contents

Ahmed Morsi: Poet of Love and Conscience

Poet Ahmed Morsi represents a unique model in Arabic poetry, combining depth of meaning with the beauty of artistic formulation. His creations vary between classical and colloquial poetry and children's poetry, in addition to romantic poetry that highlights his ability to portray human feelings in a sophisticated and influential style.

His Romantic Poetic Works: A Journey into the World of Emotion

Love and passion form a central theme in five of his romantic collections, which bear a unique imprint:

1. O You Who Were My Love: A collection of poems in which he recalls nostalgia for memories of old love and describes the beauty of the romantic relationship in a moving style.
2. The fragrance of memories: It evokes the immortal moments of love that left an indelible mark on the soul.
3. Tehi Dalalan: Celebrating feminine beauty and charm that captivates hearts.
4. Seagulls of Longing: He paints a poetic painting full of feelings of nostalgia and longing with a transparent spirit.
5. It combines the inner music of poetry and the images of nostalgia, the deep-sounding nightingales that sing of love and beauty.

He published 14 poetry collections, including:

Eight collections in classical Arabic, such as

1. Nightingales released by nostalgia
2. The scent of memories

If I Live Longer

******

If I were to live much longer,

My love to you would be so stronger,

For you dwell in the depth of my heart,

So sweet, you seem like honey, and smart.

When I close my eyes to see you,

Distant planets appear in a charming view.

Your lips also seem like the full round moon,

Your face is like the dawn or the sun at noon.

Like the scent of roses when we meet together,

When we whisper to the breeze, and love each other.

When we see that cloud, which comes with rain,

When the flutes of love play our tunes again.

When the sun of hopes does never change,

Yet, life will continue with us. How strange!

I became too drunk with the ecstasy of love

To see your beauty more, my sweet little dove.

What a lovely angel you ever seem to me!

As innocent as a child so chaste to see!

Despite long years your love will remain,

As gentle as breeze as it touches a mountain.

Like birds that swagger and fly all around,

Singing melodious songs with their beautiful sound.

You are, in my life, like a sparkling light,

Though my eyes closed, I would stay up the night.

I became as jealous as my heart that adored you,

My longing to meet you will never change, too.

I write many verses, and melt with wine,

When I drink from the cup of your love at the shrine.

For your love is still as fragrant as a rose,

Your face as bright as the moon in its pose.

When you are away, I fly to you so fast

As a soaring bird, as an arrow you did cast.

I wander in my path like the waves in the sea,

Like the beating of my heart, like the shaking of the tree.

I live a blessed time with your sweet scent,

My longing for you with my love will melt,

So, come like flowers and be never late,

Your love is a destiny, as you are my fate.

Your love is a perfume that sweetens my days,

With musk and amber from which love sprays.

I swear that you are like the far sundown,

Your eyelashes rimmed with kohl, dark brown.

I speak to the stars with my obedient heart,

I recall my memories when I come and depart.

I loved you like a phantom that haunted my dreams,

As delicate and amazing as it always seems.

Your love within my soul is sublime and great,

When asked by friends, I say, it is my fate.

The Roses of Sweethearts

******

O roses, love is nothing but a melody for a song,

To which we aspire to hear for long.

You give your fragrance to lovers who cry

And wipe their tears of longing from the eye.

Your perfumes will remain as long as they flow

With love, in our hearts, which is aglow.

If ever anguish dwells in hearts like a thorn,

A new dawn will come as a new baby, born.

If we plant love among all the lovers,

It will soon blossom like such odorous flowers.

Life might seem barren and sterile,

Yet, it would revive with water of the Nile.

I have come to sow roses and lilies

In such heart that my all passions carries.

So dance with my song like a tall palm tree

That shakes in the wind to throw dates on me.

The nature of roses when you give them love,

Like a lovely bright dawn that looms from above.

They grant you their radiance when they shine

To light all the spheres, and so never pine.

Their thorns, like spears, prick when you touch.

Yet, they have fragrance you will like so much.

Roses, like a child with a big smile, rise

To embrace a warm heart for fear of demise.

Love is like a river whose banks have no end,

And ever looks smart with passion that we send.

So plant lovely roses that adorn every park

To shade us with leaves, and leave a good mark.

Once you get to know the nature of roses

And taste such melodies that love exposes,

You will live in bliss and joy forever,

And forget all cares that make you shiver.

So come to my city, O bearer of scent!

And look for lovers who were for long absent.

Never neglect flowers lest they all wither,

For love with passion should ever come together.

Not the beauty of eyes that capture your heart,

But caring your partner with love, so smart.

Then you see the whole universe spacious and vast,

And love becomes eternal, as long as you last.

From such fragrant flowers, weave your dress

And live with morals and love in bliss.

My Sweetheart

******

O balmy flower, among roses, I behold!

Since I met you, my feelings have been bold.

You show your beauty that boasts in the hill,

Like dew, to the winds, its story does tell.

How delicate you seem as you stand alone!

Like light in the breeze of a new dawn.

Was my heart right that loved you so much?

Or these were the signs of passion as such?

The niche of beauty I found in your heart.

With arrows of love, towards me, you would dart.

My sweetheart, you are like that morn, so bright

With your face that shines to give us light.

My feelings in the sea of passions do flow,

Whose waves run after the breeze that go.

They fold all the distances long under their feet,

And yearn for their lover in order to meet

In the garden of passions, among all the trees

Whose twigs are moved by the gentle breeze.

Life becomes bitter when you leave and depart,

And roses die soon on the candle of the heart.

Yet, love in my ribs dwells as you see

And tells about the passions you gifted to me.

Your beauty makes me go under its spell,

And so your charm bewitches me as well.

What shall I say if my passions would appear

To sweep my heart with love I never bear?

I never knew for once that I would ever dream

Of loving such eyes whose cunning I esteem.

But my love came to me like a fast cloud

That would, after rain, come and strut around.

O my babe, my bliss, you are mine,

On the love book, you put your first line.

My spirit will to you my love secret reveal

So that my deep bleeding wounds can heal.

All the planets of love would dance with you;

They look like scattered drops of dew.

O my flower, your charm can exceed

All other women whose beauty I never heed.

Like the moon light when it shines will cover

All the stars around that hide and shiver!

The Love Alphabet

******

I thought of drawing a lovely rose,

And adorn the paper with my prose.

I poured some perfume in my ink

To write my poems and all what I think.

But people look to what I write,

I left the page so blank and white.

I kept thinking what to say

Until the morn of the next day.

At sunrise, my orchard can reveal:

Roses have the power to cure and heal.

So in my poems all perfumes I would add,

To write my dedication, I was very glad.

I played love melodies with all my strings,

Then put them all on the flying birds' wings.

I waited for the news so that I might read

Something about her, for I am in bad need.

Should I, all my poetry for roses, dedicate?

For a dumb love flower, I confine my fate?

Does my rose smell aromatic in its bower,

And dance for love with every flower?

So all my question, you have to respond,

To tell me in public: "Of her you are fond."

My babe's name is written in the first line

With my love alphabet, to be beside mine.

You sent your flowers, my love, to guide me,

The symbol of lovers, for all who can see.

O mistress, who looks gorgeous in this life,

You pine with love and suffer much strife.

You pick many roses, some pink and red,

Then offer them to me to put on my bed.

Yet thorns prick your palms that would bleed

They dance with roses to mock the weed.

Each color of rose has a different meaning

In lovers' language, whose hearts are beating.

Its scent is the echo in every space

When you smell it, so shines your face.

You are my realm, in which I rule,

And read my poetry from heart to soul.

I never loved a woman but you, my dear.

Yet messages to lovers I used to bear.

With you, I own this world, so wide,

And on the dreams' horses, I can ride.

The last line

******

Care not when you write your love's last line;

Cut off the thread between your heart and mine.

For now, I have no memories of you anymore,

As age erased in silence all that of yore.

Carve all your wishes on my tender heart,

What is worthy in life if you depart?

We had a long journey together in the past,

With love and passions that long did last.

How much we poured tears out of desire,

And so hearts were scorched in the desert fire.

Pick up all the memories that may remain

Of our past days and throw on the plain.

On the ruins of our house, spray your scent

A long time within its walls, we have spent.

Yesterday, I was the master of all my affairs,

Now, humiliated by this fate that never cares.

Nothing but love in your heart I could see,

So why did you throw it into the mighty sea?

Fear not such memories that soon will perish.

Nothing is left of them, as all will vanish.

We will leave our abode in hasty footsteps,

To bury dead hearts as the sun does eclipse.

Leave me as you wish. Is that your dream?

To read my death on the water of your stream?

Thrust your arrow hard in my thirsty heart,

Clothe it in white shrouds and bury it; start

In the land where it used to walk all around

Like a blind old man lost on the mound.

Say not that my heart sought once your shade

From such blazing fire, the sun had made.

In the language of love, two opposites meet.

How does a sexy dress sweep off your feet?

Thus love melts away and never comes back,

When our passions die, we lose our track.

No longer will we meet in such rainy days,

When lovers used to sit on their love ways.

Tell them: our hearts never ceased to bleed,

Did they went blind? So love could not read.

Say not how many deep wounds we got,

Before passions died. What a bad, sad lot!

Then on the ruins of your dead heart,

Take your dreams for a new, fresh start

In our long journey, we face much strife,

How fast and short passes our life!

Never Apologize

******

Never apologize to me or give an excuse;

Your betrayal has shaken me, as you me abuse.

You have offered yourself on me, all for free.

Yet I was not as Joseph, the prophet, in piety.

All the evidence of your fouls you try to hide;

You ignited a blazing fire that would never subside.

You dried up the wellspring of bygone memories,

How ugly, the love you never knew, how bad it is!

For breaking your promises, I would not forgive.

Immoral is betrayal in the vows that you give.

You were not as loyal as my close friend,

So, hasten to take off my soul in the end.

The winds would slap me and rip my coats,

Be not ashamed of your puzzled thoughts.

How did you spill the pure blood of my soul?

How did we both wake up to this bitter gall?

Every day, I see you with lovers that you share

Your passions and whims with; so never swear.

Your panicked bed, which I saw, was a raging fire,

While you both were in your hot desire.

Where is your pledge to me? It was long gone!

I heard you both before you were really done.

Be not so kind to me, and thrust your sharp arrow,

Play your tune at my grave that is narrow.

Know that all eagerness within me has died,

Your chains in my hands have also been untied.

O my heart, cease to write all your verse,

As my soul has just ceased to give any pulse.

After all my fears had faded, O my poor heart!

She tricked me as a whore who played her foul part.

In reality, your love is not such good or fair;

From the cup of bitterness, I sip and share.

Now all the ears of wheat are burning like dry hay,

So with the evening, O you reckless, please go away.

I begged you with tears running from my eyes

To quit the false fortress of your ugly lies.

Dance over graves to sing your all melodies;

Bid me farewell, how bad your fake apology is!

You are an arrow stabbed in my bleeding vein;

And a prick of conscience that you may feign.

You defiled my running stream, so pure and chaste.

Therefore, to my repentance I seek and haste.

I read from the Holy Qur'an so many verses;

And prayed to my God to seek His forgiveness.

O You Who were My Love

******

Were you the start of my entire story?

Were you in my poetry its best melody?

Or were you the embers of my end?

You were not my love that arrows send

In the ribs to kill my poor heart;

I kept your covenant on my part

To go on the way of your passions.

How much did I hear of your confessions!

Think not that my heart is feeble or so frail

Or my eyes with tears like nectar for you bewail.

As on this day my story has begun,

As the years of my life with anguish have run.

Yet, your treachery has overthrown me,

It is like a volcano that erupts in the sea.

It blows up whatever stands on its way.

You caused me to suffer wounds all day.

You rejected me, wronged me, and hurt;

Now, never apologize as you sold me short.

Your betrayal caused my sorrow;

You claimed that some girls you did follow;

You forgot that I craved you like a boat,

O the river of love did quickly float.

Did the girls really come to visit you?

Or is it a lover who yearns for you?

Who comes to you on the nearest date,

To be with you in the first seat.

He shares you love, drink and talk;

Observes your breath, feelings as you walk;

Whispers in your hands; melts in your eyes;

Longs for your lips; in eyebrows lies;

What about the silk shawl that you wear

Intentionally on your shoulders, smart and fair?

The showers of perfume that have strong smell,

Which about the treachery of your passions tell.

You let him drink from the same cup of love,

And sip our passions that lift us above.

How oft does he call to drink from your wine?

In your feminine voice, said," Here you will be mine."

You killed me and shed my blood with words;

You broke my heart and increased my wounds.

Your treachery made your eyes blind;

Disgrace on your eyebrows I did find.

And shame appeared on each cheek.

"Stop it" I said, amazed, as I did shriek

Everyone out there my secret can tell,

That I let your heart between my ribs dwell.

I willingly give my life to the sea of tears.

I will tell the dreams all about my fears.

I will say all about you to my days

That you betrayed me by all ways;

Therefore, I now reject all your love

Even if my longing to you I may give.

You have deceived me told me lies, too.

And said that all the girls came to you.

My Sparrow Died

******

Alas! My sparrow has sadly perished!

Since the longing within me vanished.

So my burning heart has died,

And all its secrets in the sea did hide.

How oft did it shelter in my porch?

Every once in a while it used to search

For a place to chant and dance in joy,

To be for lovers their best envoy.

One day it came and cried to me;

It was groaning in severe misery.

I said, "O sparrow! Please, tell me.

Were you snared by damn treachery?"

It said, "Love is but a mirage, so vile.

It keeps fading every once and a while."

Then love is gone and forever lost,

I lived in jail all days that passed.

My heart has died in the traitors' fort.

The trees around me have died short.

The heart of Jasmin has also gone,

The light went out in my bright sun.

So I hate such time when you denied my love

Whose river dried up, and killed my dove.

It was long ago, as years had elapsed

In my secure nest, the light has collapsed.

The guard of love has blocked my vein.

So the pulse stopped as my heart did wane.

In the maze of sand, my days have parted.

They all have gone in the paths of the departed.

My soul bid farewell to the companion of the way

And left him stumbling and going astray.

Ask not if once you were totally lost

With me in a caravan in a land so waste.

You were but tears in my weeping eyes.

You blocked the sun that used to rise.

If you see someone now other than me

Walk on the long paths of doubt and query,

Build a nest of love, then quickly quit.

Forget the miserable days, which I will forget.

O sparrow, made of water and mud,

Leave love that runs in your blood.

I have my love kingdom, so vast and great,

Without those who envy you or hate.

You no longer sings your wonted tune

To us who were left behind on the dune.

O bird who disappeared in grief and misery!

A flock of birds reported your tragedy.